THE
GRATITUDE
EXPLORER
WORKBOOK

Guided Practices, Meditations, and Reflections
for Cultivating Gratefulness in Daily Life

KRISTI NELSON

A Network for Grateful Living

Storey Publishing

The mission of Storey Publishing is to serve our customers by publishing practical information that encourages personal independence in harmony with the environment.

Edited by Liz Bevilacqua and Sarah Guare
Art direction and book design by
   Alethea Morrison
Text production by Liseann Karandisecky
Cover watercolors by © Nomoco, back-
   grounds (f. & b.) and © Katie Eberts,
   lotus, spine, sticker, postcard, star
Interior watercolors by © Katie Eberts,
   with additional watercolors by Clikchic
   Designs

Portions of the text have been adapted
from *Wake Up Grateful* by Kristi Nelson
(Storey Publishing, 2020) and *Everyday
Gratitude* by A Network for Grateful Living (Storey Publishing, 2018).

Storey books are available at special
discounts when purchased in bulk for
premiums and sales promotions as well as
for fund-raising or educational use. Special
editions or book excerpts can also be
created to specification. For details, please
call 800-827-8673, or send an email to
sales@storey.com.

Storey Publishing
210 MASS MoCA Way
North Adams, MA 01247
storey.com

Printed in China by Shenzhen Reliance
   Printing Co. Ltd.
10 9 8 7 6 5 4 3 2 1

QUOTE SOURCES

Brunton, Paul. *The Notebooks of Paul Brunton:
   A Creative Synthesis of Eastern and Western
   Ideas, vol. 1: Perspectives: The Timeless Way of
   Wisdom* (Larson Publications, 1984).
Clendenin, Dan, "Giving Thanks in an Age of
   Entitlement," *Journey with Jesus: Notes to
   Myself*, November 25, 2002.
Huber, Cheri, *How You Do Anything Is How You
   Do Everything: A Workbook* (Keep It Simple,
   1998).
Kornfield, Jack, *Buddha's Little Instruction Book*
   (Bantam, 1994).
Nepo, Mark, *The Book of Awakening* © 2020,
   2011, 2000 reprinted by permission of Red
   Wheel/Weiser, LLC Newburyport, MA
   www.redwheelweiser.com.
Remen, Rachel Naomi, *Kitchen Table Wisdom:
   Stories That Heal* (Riverhead, 1996).
Steindl-Rast, David, *Gratefulness, the Heart of
   Prayer: An Approach to Life in Fullness*
   (Paulist Press, 1984).

CONTENTS

Every Day Is an Opportunity for Exploration, 5

PART 1: Become Present, 9

PART 2: Seek Perspective, 49

PART 3: Awaken Possibility, 89

Gratitude Extras, 128
Star Stickers
Affirmation Stickers
Bookmarks
Postcards
Mini Quote Cards
Conversation Starters

GRATEFULNESS IS THE GALLANTRY OF A HEART READY TO RISE TO THE OPPORTUNITY A GIVEN MOMENT OFFERS.

BROTHER DAVID STEINDL-RAST

EVERY DAY IS
AN OPPORTUNITY
FOR EXPLORATION

Life lays out a banquet of opportunities for you to engage in living gratefully. All the ingredients of grateful living are available to you, and each day is yours to make a bountiful feast. Life delivers opportunities in every moment: drinking tea, driving, making a meal, engaging in a conversation, going on a walk, sitting at your desk, taking care of someone, or brushing your teeth. There are as many ways to live gratefully as there are moments in the day. It can be elegantly simple—so, begin wherever you are.

To be present to your life as it unfolds, to occupy each moment with a grateful heart, and to notice with curiosity what is happening inside and around you—all this delivers the possibility of contentment and joy. And all of it is facilitated by practice. It may seem odd that you would need to "practice" being available to life, but where and how you offer your attention shapes the ways you live your moments, and therefore how you experience life. Practice makes your moments more intentional and vivid—and it allows you to be more available to what matters most to you in life.

You will notice that simply making a commitment to grateful living as a practice in and of itself sends vital messages to your cells, your mind, your heart, and those around you. These messages help remind you to savor the life you have and be more available for its gifts. Committing to living gratefully helps reveal all the reasons you have to be thankful—waking you up to things you may have never noticed before and many you may have taken for granted. It opens your senses wider, focuses your awareness more intently, and orients you toward appreciation. It transforms how you see and relate to the people and the world around you, allowing greater curiosity, kindness, and concern.

Grateful living is experienced and expressed in how you live the life you have. This life. Here and now. In the midst of any moment, if you simply pause to more fully notice and savor it before carrying on, this is grateful living in practice.

Become Present, Seek Perspective, and Awaken Possibility

Gratitude wakes you up to what matters. It helps you be aware of all that is sufficient and abundant in your life. It keeps you alert to meaningful truths. It supports your capacity to live with appreciation, and it makes you feel more alive.

Practicing grateful living helps you become more mindful of opportunities, and it shifts your awareness to the things that awaken and serve you. It helps guide your heart and focus your mind on gratitude for the simple gift of your life. Many of us need to cultivate methods and practices to connect with or reinvigorate grateful awareness when it is not readily accessible. Cultivation harnesses the energy of our intentions. Just as we can cultivate a bountiful flower or vegetable garden, we can cultivate qualities in our lives that we desire and that will serve our lives and the lives of those around us. What we nourish with our attention will nourish us in turn.

The practice of introducing simple moments and experiences of gratefulness into your day is profound. When you remind yourself of this practice throughout the day and string these moments together, you discover that these subtle internal shifts impact your sense of well-being. The commitment to living gratefully itself will yield tangible gifts and guide you, over time, to greater joy and peace—both for yourself and others. Trust this. And keep returning to your grateful intentions. For a deeper dive into the principles and philosophies in these pages, read the book from which this workbook draws its inspiration: *Wake Up Grateful*. And for more inspirational quotes, look for our book *Everyday Gratitude*.

STAR PROMPTS AND TOOLS

Throughout the pages you will see positive statements that reflect practices we can all do, such as "I allowed myself to slow down." We've included sheets of colorful star stickers in the back so you can reward your own progress. At the back, you will also find other pop-out tools to aid your gratitude practice: affirmation stickers, bookmarks, postcards and mini quote cards, and conversation starters. Have fun exploring.

PART 1

BECOME PRESENT

Presence allows you to be alert to the wonder
and fullness of your life and
opens you to perspective.

Whenever you wonder how you might access gratefulness in a given moment, try this: Simply return to awareness of your breath—inhale and exhale gratefully. Recognize the fact of your aliveness. Tune in to your body as it breathes for you. Feel appreciation for the moment. Invite your heart to soften in gratitude for the opportunity that life is offering you in this moment. Notice the ways that this is enough.

BECOME FULLY PRESENT

Take a few minutes to focus on becoming fully present to the moment as it is. Use your breath and your senses to simply notice wherever and however you are. Even one conscious breath can deepen or shift your experience. Pause for greater presence as many times in the day as you can.

» Pausing for stillness, I am aware . . .

_____

_____

_____

» Taking a deep breath, I connect with . . .

_____

_____

_____

_____

» Tuning into my body, I feel . . .

_____

_____

_____

_____

» Embracing silence, I hear . . .

_____

_____

_____

_____

» Slowing down, I notice . . .

_____

_____

_____

_____

_____

_____

_____

_____

» Paying attention, I smell . . .

_____

_____

_____

_____

_____

_____

_____

_____

» Pausing where I am, I see . . .

_____

_____

_____

_____

_____

_____

_____

_____

I ALLOWED MYSELF TO
SLOW DOWN.

★ ★ ★

★ ★ ★

★ ★ ★

★ ★ ★

What wonders can I enjoy without spending a dime or
going to distant places?

The WORLD IS A PLACE WHERE THE EXTRAORDINARY CAN SIT JUST BESIDE THE ORDINARY WITH THE THINNEST OF BOUNDARIES.

JODI PICOULT

WAKE UP GRATEFUL

When you wake up, before getting out of bed, pause to notice and appreciate at least three things you can already be grateful for. For example: *My lungs are working. My eyes can open. There are people I love.* Think of things that you don't have to earn or receive from anyone else—things you are already receiving from life before doing anything. This is a powerful practice to greet each day and helps you to feel centered in the privilege and gifts of life.

DATE:_____ /_____ /_____

» As I wake, I am grateful for . . .

_____

_____

_____

_____

_____

DATE:_____ /_____ /_____

» As I wake, I am grateful for . . .

_____

_____

_____

_____

_____

_____

DATE:_____ /_____ /_____

» As I wake, I am grateful for . . .

_____

_____

_____

_____

_____

_____

_____

DATE:_____ /_____ /_____

» As I wake, I am grateful for . . .

_____

_____

_____

_____

_____

_____

_____

DATE:_____ /_____ /_____

» As I wake, I am grateful for . . .

_____

_____

_____

_____

_____

_____

_____

I APPRECIATED THREE THINGS BEFORE I STARTED MY DAY.

★ ★ ★

★ ★ ★

★ ★ ★

★ ★ ★

BE INSIGHT-FULL

When you quiet the voices and noise inside and around you, you open up to the wise guidance that is always available. Create a regular practice to tune in to your own core intelligence—the wellspring that manifests as heart guidance, gut instinct, and intuition. There is endless wisdom waiting for you in every moment.

» When I still myself to listen within, what wisdom emerges?

_____

_____

_____

_____

_____

_____

_____

_____

_____

_____

_____

_____

_____

_____

_____

_____

_____

_____

_____

_____

LET US ACCEPT THE INVITATION, EVER-OPEN, FROM THE **STILLNESS**, TASTE ITS EXQUISITE SWEETNESS, AND HEED ITS SILENT INSTRUCTION.

PAUL BRUNTON

GO TO BED GRATEFUL

Each night before you go to sleep, reflect on some of the things for which you are grateful. Let these things float through your mind and calm your body. Write down at least three things that matter to you. Fall asleep gratefully.

DATE:_____ /_____ /_____

» As I fall asleep, I am grateful for . . .

_____

_____

_____

_____

_____

_____

DATE:_____ /_____ /_____

» As I fall asleep, I am grateful for . . .

_____

_____

_____

_____

_____

_____

_____

DATE:_____ /_____ /_____

» As I fall asleep, I am grateful for . . .

_____

_____

_____

_____

_____

_____

_____

_____

DATE:_____ /_____ /_____

» As I fall asleep, I am grateful for . . .

_____

_____

_____

_____

_____

_____

_____

DATE:_____ /_____ /_____

» As I fall asleep, I am grateful for . . .

_____

_____

_____

_____

_____

_____

_____

_____

I APPRECIATED THREE THINGS AT THE END OF THE DAY.

★ ★ ★

★ ★ ★

★ ★ ★

★ ★ ★

THANKS
TO THE
HUMAN HEART
BY WHICH
WE LIVE,
THANKS TO ITS
TENDERNESS,
ITS JOYS, AND FEARS

WILLIAM WORDSWORTH

SEE EMOTIONS AS ENERGY IN MOTION

Close your eyes and take a few deep breaths. Notice an emotion that is in the background of your direct attention, a feeling asking for recognition. Invite it into your awareness and welcome it by name: *Hello, _____*. Simply acknowledging and naming your feelings can help them soften and have less of a charge. Practice greeting this same feeling by name with each exhale until another feeling enters your awareness. Welcome it in as you gently allow the first emotion to move on. Notice and appreciate that feelings are always in motion, all the more so when you acknowledge them and let them go.

» Hello, _____

» Hello, _____

» Hello, _____

» Hello, _____

» Hello, _____

» Hello, _____

» Hello, _____

» Hello, _____

» Hello, _____

» Hello, _____

» Hello, _____

» Hello, _____

I MADE ROOM FOR ALL MY FEELINGS, WITHOUT JUDGMENT.

WAIT WITHOUT WAITING

Turn all of the "waiting" moments of the day into moments of heightened awareness. Try to be fully present in these instances to what is happening around and within you. Notice that time "between" things can be a huge gift. Enjoy an unexpected opportunity to pause in your day.

» What opportunities do I have to practice "waiting without waiting"?

_____

_____

_____

_____

_____

_____

_____

_____

_____

_____

_____

_____

_____

I SPENT SOME "WAITING MOMENTS" IN PRESENCE AND APPRECIATION.

★ ★ ★ ★ ★ ★

NOTICE THE MIRACLE OF BREATH

Practice pausing throughout the day to breathe deeply: slowly, all the way in and all the way out. Now notice how your breathing takes care of itself . . . rhythmically moving through you about 23,000 times per day, keeping you alive and vital. Commit to not taking this miracle for granted.

» What feelings and thoughts arise in me when I tune in to the wonder of my living body?

FIND MYSTERY

Sit comfortably and take time to notice your breath. Allow your next exhale to take you into a place of peace with simply being present in your body. Right now you do not need to know, predict, or guarantee anything. Shift your intention to notice the presence of mystery. Take whatever time you need to settle into this awareness. Notice if images, sensations, or feelings arise. Does mystery have an essence or image for you? If so, invite yourself to feel its shape, its heft, its promise. Everything in your life beyond this moment is held in this place. Sit for a few minutes and let yourself ponder the presence of mystery, and your presence with it.

» What holds mystery? How does mystery hold me?

_____

_____

_____

_____

_____

_____

_____

_____

_____

_____

I WAS PRESENT TO MYSTERY TODAY.

★ ★ ★ ★ ★ ★

TO LIVE IS SO STARTLING, IT LEAVES BUT LITTLE ROOM FOR OTHER OCCUPATIONS.

EMILY DICKINSON

DELIGHT IN YOUR SENSES

As physical beings, we use our senses to experience life. How often do you find yourself sleepwalking through a day, and then catch sight of something—a beautiful bird, flower, or smiling face—and your heart wakes up? The sound of your favorite music can crack you open. A certain smell or taste can make buried memories surface. Your senses have a profound power to stir up positive sensation and memory. These pleasures can be potent medicine, especially if you have been wounded by pain or illness.

Remember your senses and how they deliver pleasure and blessing for yourself and others. Give gifts that open the senses.

» Sensations that delight me . . .

\
\
\
\
\
\

» Sounds that delight me . . .

\
\
\
\
\
\
\

» Sights that delight me . . .

_____

_____

_____

_____

_____

_____

_____

_____

_____

» Smells that delight me . . .

_____

_____

_____

_____

_____

_____

_____

_____

» Tastes that delight me . . .

_____

_____

_____

_____

_____

_____

_____

_____

_____

I GRATEFULLY OPENED TO MY SENSES TODAY.

★ ★ ★

★ ★ ★

★ ★ ★

★ ★ ★

ABSORB ALL THE GOODNESS

If you make an effort to fully enjoy pleasing experiences, you will be better equipped to face the challenging times in your life. Instead of distracting yourself from a pleasurable moment, go into super-soak mode and absorb every bit of its goodness. Let the blessings of an enjoyable moment saturate your cells. Occupy it fully. Create such a powerful reservoir of pleasure that it can carry you through challenging times.

When you find yourself feeling grateful, keep your mind focused on that feeling and really take it all in.

» What experiences in life often bring me pleasure? What do I love about them?

_____

_____

_____

_____

_____

_____

_____

_____

_____

_____

_____

_____

I ALLOWED MYSELF TO LEAN FULLY INTO A PLEASING MOMENT.

★ ★ ★ ★ ★ ★

BE YOURSELF WITH ABANDON

Your capacity to experience pleasure rests in your ability to be comfortable with who you are. From a place of self-acceptance, you can better notice beauty and celebrate life through all of your senses and see yourself as an essential part of the whole. You can play, rest, laugh, and create with abandon. By not needing to do more and be more, you open the doors to the fullness of enjoyment.

Notice more of the pleasures in being exactly who you are. Embrace your quirks and let them show more, laugh at yourself, and find the occasion to laud your humanity, with love.

» What are 10 quirks I love about myself?

1. I love _____

2. I love _____

3. I love _____

4. I love _____

5. I love _____

6. I love _____

7. I love _____

8. I love _____

9. I love _____

10. I love _____

I LOVED MYSELF WITH ABANDON TODAY.

★ ★ ★ ★ ★ ★

How can I honor the preciousness of this day?

DATE:_____ /_____ /_____

_____

_____

_____

_____

_____

_____

How can I honor the preciousness of this day?

DATE:_____ /_____ /_____

_____

_____

_____

_____

_____

_____

How can I honor the preciousness of this day?

DATE:_____ /_____ /_____

_____

_____

_____

_____

_____

_____

JUST TO BE

IS A
BLESSING.
JUST TO
LIVE IS
HOLY.

RABBI ABRAHAM JOSHUA HESCHEL

GRATITUDE PLACES YOU IN THE ENERGY FIELD OF PLENTITUDE. GLOW WITH GRATITUDE AND SEE HOW AWE AND JOY WILL MAKE THEIR HOME IN YOU.

MICHAEL BERNARD BECKWITH

EMBODY GRATITUDE

Take a few slow breaths as you settle into a seated position. As your mind quiets, close your eyes and imagine sitting with gratitude and reverence for your body. See yourself embodying a posture that totally treasures your body, exactly as it is. What does it look like? How does it feel? Make adjustments in the way that you are sitting so as to occupy this embodiment of gratitude. Where do your hands want to be placed? How is your spine? Does your head change position? Experiment with subtle shifts until you find a posture that reflects a treasuring of your body. Take a few more breaths and notice what arises. Open your eyes and offer yourself some appreciation. As you observe and experience your body throughout the day, try to let it move gratefully.

» How does gratitude change how I hold and carry my body?
  What changes inside me and around me when I embody gratitude?

BE WITH YOURSELF AS YOU WOULD BE WITH OTHERS

We often give our best advice to people when they are facing challenging emotions. Often our best selves rise to the occasion, and we share what we hold as sacred. We speak from the heart of our true beliefs and we offer kindness and compassion to others. If we are able to turn this same sacred appreciation toward ourselves, we can align with what we stand for.

Make a real effort to give yourself the focused emotional attention that you offer others. Your well-being will benefit greatly when you tend yourself with such appreciation and care.

» What challenging emotions have I felt recently?
  What appreciative care could I give myself?

» What does my spirit need right now?

_____

_____

_____

_____

_____

_____

_____

_____

» What parts of myself want to be held with empathy today?

_____

_____

_____

_____

_____

_____

_____

_____

_____

_____

HARVEST LOVE FROM LOSS

Think of a person you love whose loss you suffered long enough ago that thinking about their absence does not feel overly acute. Write a list of 10 things that wake up your heart when you think of them—special memories, gifts you received, laughs you shared, meaning that they brought, qualities you cherished.

When you fill yourself with gratitude, even if it feels particularly poignant, you honor yourself, your connection, and the person you miss. Let your heart ride on a sweet wave of grateful love in the present moment.

» When I remember my beloved, my heart is moved by the thought of:

1. _____

2. _____

3. _____

4. _____

5. _____

6. _____

7. _____

8. _____

9. _____

10. _____

» When you are done, speak each memory aloud, saying "I am grateful to remember" before each one.

JOY IS THE GIFT OF LOVE. GRIEF IS THE PRICE OF LOVE.

VALARIE KAUR

CELEBRATE BEING BOTH BROKEN AND WHOLE

You are alive, and you have no idea how long this is going to be true. You live every day inside this great mystery, and yet it can be challenging to acknowledge regularly. Denying or ignoring the fact of your impermanence keeps you from the work of befriending your body. Your body deserves to be treasured, now. It wants to be celebrated as it is—broken and whole. You give yourself an irreplaceable gift when you praise your body every day as a temporary, extraordinary temple that offers you the benefit of being alive.

Let yourself be drawn into the miraculous mystery of your body in this moment. It carries you with such generosity and commitment in the face of all its unknowns. Live as a celebration of this love.

» What aspect of my body do I feel most grateful for in this moment and why?

_____

_____

_____

_____

_____

_____

_____

_____

_____

_____

_____

_____

» What does my body need to feel nourished?

_____

_____

_____

_____

_____

_____

_____

» What does my body need to feel rested?

_____

_____

_____

_____

_____

_____

_____

» What does my body need to feel energized?

_____

_____

_____

_____

_____

_____

_____

I CELEBRATED AND CARED FOR
MY BODY AS IT IS.

★ ★ ★

★ ★ ★

★ ★ ★

★ ★ ★

LISTEN WITH PRESENCE

When you are talking with someone, you might believe you are fully present, but if you repeatedly invite yourself to drop in a little deeper, you can go to unexpected levels. Take a breath or two to be more wholly available. Purposefully release thoughts not related to the interaction and notice what becomes accessible when you bring all your attention to the moment.

Experiment with holding eye contact and notice how you can listen with your eyes as well as your ears. Tune in to what is being said, and really hear it. Let yourself be impacted by what you hear. Listen to listen. Invite your heart to become more grateful. If you find yourself distracted, invite yourself to come back into appreciative presence. Keep dropping deeper. It works wonders. You might even experiment with using this presence practice with someone you are meeting for the first time and notice what unfolds in your connection.

» When I listen gratefully to a friend or stranger, what do I hear? What do I experience? How does it impact my relationship with this person?

BEAUTY IS THE HARVEST OF PRESENCE.

DAVID WHYTE

REDUCE YOUR CHANCES FOR REGRET

Every time you allow yourself to be deeply touched in a relationship, you reduce the chance for regret. If you live as though nothing is promised, you cultivate the ability to be fully present with your vulnerability and therefore with others. You can recognize the ever-present possibility that moments of connection may not come again, and so make them truly matter. Show up with your heart open, knowing that it costs you nothing and affords you everything.

Think about the ways that you connect with people—each one is an opening for meaning-making. Truly open all of your senses and be fully present. Say something meaningful and sincere. Take the time to make a real connection. Make it last. You will never regret it.

» How would I connect with my loved ones if I knew this was our last time together?

_____

_____

_____

_____

_____

_____

_____

_____

_____

_____

_____

I GREETED SOMEONE WITH LOVE AND APPRECIATION.

★ ★ ★ ★ ★ ★

I SAID GOODBYE WITH LOVE AND APPRECIATION.

★ ★ ★ ★ ★ ★

I LISTENED WITH LOVE AND APPRECIATION.

★ ★ ★ ★ ★ ★

I HUGGED SOMEONE WITH MY WHOLE SELF.

★ ★ ★ ★ ★ ★

I GAVE MEANINGFUL COMPLIMENTS OR SUPPORT TODAY.

★ ★ ★ ★ ★ ★

TUNE IN TO MAGNIFICENCE

We too often take natural beauty for granted. Stuck in feeling deprived or disappointed by life, we walk by the Earth's splendor without noticing. Meanwhile, nature is busy every moment creating magnificence that brings us hope and delights our senses. A sunrise and birdsong start our day, a tree growing through pavement moves us to hope, perennials commit to us even if we move away, and plants say "breathe" and make it all possible. Our senses attune us to creation, creativity, and celebration. How much more pleasure could we want? How much more alive could we feel?

Stop to look for nature's tenacity and magnificence more often. Look up. Look down. Look out. When you discover it, make time to take it in more deeply. Be still and let yourself be moved.

» What aspects or parts of nature make my soul come alive?

_____

_____

_____

_____

_____

_____

_____

_____

_____

_____

_____

_____

IN ALL THINGS OF **NATURE** THERE IS SOMETHING OF THE **MARVELOUS.**

ARISTOTLE

All that is necessary to AWAKEN to yourself as the RADIANT EMPTINESS OF SPIRIT is to stop SEEKING SOMETHING MORE OR BETTER OR DIFFERENT, AND TO TURN YOUR ATTENTION INWARD TO THE AWAKE SILENCE THAT YOU ARE.

ADYASHANTI

What happens when I stop believing that something more and different will make my life better?

PART 2

SEEK PERSPECTIVE

Perspective expands your experience of life, allowing for greater appreciation of the opportunities available to you, and opens you to possibility.

When you see the ordinary as extraordinary and take nothing for granted, you can turn your life into a wellspring of abundance. If you look at everything with appreciative eyes, you are likely to be overwhelmed by the amazing gifts at your fingertips, the abundance of how much is in service to your life. Awakening to the great good fortune that is yours can stop the feeling of needing more. The practice of fully appreciating what is already in front of you can be a joyful long-term engagement. You might find that you already have all the abundance that you envied, craved, or thought you needed.

SHIFT FROM OBLIGATION TO OPPORTUNITY

Throughout your day, catch yourself whenever you think, "I have to . . ." and try to substitute with "I get to." Notice how different it feels to think that you get to do something. How does this shift the energy you bring to each task? You can also try adding, "because I can" to the end of your "get-to" statements. This can help you see your tasks as privileges you may not have always had and may not always have in the future, and that many people do not have at all. Begin to notice how much other people use obligated language in day-to-day conversations. Experiment with seeing and claiming your responsibilities and obligations as privileges and opportunities.

DATE:_____ /_____ /_____

» What are at least five things I have to do this week?

I have to _____

I have to _____

I have to _____

I have to _____

I have to _____

» *After you list them, cross out "I have to" and write "I get to" in front of each item.*

I SHIFTED MY PERSPECTIVE AND SAW A TASK AS A PRIVILEGE TODAY.

★ ★ ★ ★ ★ ★

DATE:_____ /_____ /_____

» What are at least five things I have to do this week?

I have to _____

I have to _____

I have to _____

I have to _____

I have to _____

» *After you list them, cross out "I have to" and write "I get to" in front of each item.*

DATE:_____ /_____ /_____

» What are at least five things I have to do this week?

I have to _____

I have to _____

I have to _____

I have to _____

I have to _____

» *After you list them, cross out "I have to" and write "I get to" in front of each item.*

LOOK WITH FRESH EYES

Take at least one minute to notice some of the opportunities to be grateful that are readily available to you right now. Behold life with the openness of experiencing things as if for the very first, or the very last, time. Consider these prompts:

» Looking for reasons to be grateful, I notice . . .

_____

_____

_____

_____

_____

_____

» Looking for beauty, I see . . .

_____

_____

_____

_____

_____

_____

_____

» Looking for surprise, I discover . . .

_____

_____

_____

_____

_____

_____

_____

» Looking at my life through others'
eyes, I see . . .

_____

_____

_____

_____

_____

_____

_____

» Looking for opportunities to be
grateful, I am aware . . .

_____

_____

_____

_____

_____

_____

_____

I OPENED MYSELF TO
OPPORTUNITIES TO BE GRATEFUL.

★ ★ ★

★ ★ ★

★ ★ ★

★ ★ ★

What people, moments, or things shined light in my life today?

DATE:_____ /_____ /_____

_____

_____

_____

_____

_____

What people, moments, or things shined light in my life today?

DATE:_____ /_____ /_____

_____

_____

_____

_____

_____

What people, moments, or things shined light in my life today?

DATE:_____ /_____ /_____

_____

_____

_____

_____

_____

LIGHT
IS IN
BOTH THE
BROKEN BOTTLE
AND THE DIAMOND.

MARK NEPO

REMEMBER YOUR GIFTS

When you imagine not having the things to which you are accustomed, you can appreciate your life more. Expectations keep us asleep to life; surprise wakes us up. Cultivating a state of astonishment about your many comforts— running water, a laptop, a coffeemaker, a refrigerator, a window, or even a roof over your head—helps keep you grateful. How would life be without these privileges? Put a sticker or even a small gift bow—yes, really—on things you want to remind yourself not to forget are surprising gifts. This can also help others in your household or workplace treat things as amazing blessings rather than the same old things.

» What are some of the extraordinary aspects of my life that I tend to take for granted? How can I appreciate them more deeply?

GIVE APPRECIATIVE ATTENTION

Commit to tending one thing you may have neglected. Start with something that was a treasured item when you first got it: a houseplant, a piece of furniture, artwork, clothing, a keepsake, or a photograph. Make a practice of actively appreciating it every day to bring it back to its original appreciation-worthy state. Spend time regarding its unique beauty and detail. Notice the sentiment it evokes for you. How does this thing enrich your life? With the practice complete, choose another item.

» What happens when I offer overlooked items my appreciative attention?

I BROUGHT NEW LIFE TO SOMETHING THAT HAD BEEN FORGOTTEN.

DO IT DIFFERENTLY

Notice when you are doing something habitually. When you are in the midst of the routine, stop for one minute to bring greater awareness to what you are doing. Bring attention to your task and change one aspect so it comes more alive, and you do, too. Switch hands when brushing your teeth. Swap your usual seat at the table. Sleep on a different side of the bed, or in a different room. Take a new route to work. Try expressing generous thanks to someone you see every day. Changing a habit changes perspective, making room for new awareness. Let yourself feel the awkwardness and delight of something different. See what kinds of insights and opportunities arise when you become open to surprise.

» When I use my opposite hand to eat, I notice . . .

_____

_____

_____

_____

_____

» When I sleep on the other side of the bed, I notice . . .

_____

_____

_____

_____

_____

_____

» When I take a different route somewhere, I notice . . .

_____

_____

_____

_____

_____

_____

_____

» When I sit in a different seat at the table, I notice . . .

_____

_____

_____

_____

_____

_____

_____

» When I change what time I typically wake up or go to sleep, I notice . . .

_____

_____

_____

_____

_____

_____

_____

I GAINED INSIGHT FROM EXPLORING A DIFFERENT APPROACH TO ROUTINE.

★ ★ ★

★ ★ ★

★ ★ ★

★ ★ ★

ALL BREATHE

Close your eyes and take a few slow, full breaths. Be aware that countless trees and other plants all over the Earth have contributed to creating the oxygen that is nourishing your body through your lungs. Breathing in, remember that on every continent, in every town, everything alive is breathing with you. Breathing out, remember that plants help you breathe by taking in carbon dioxide and letting oxygen out. You are part of a benevolent cycle. When you see plants, remember they are your lifeline to aliveness. Let this reality keep you amazed and inspired.

» What changes when I recognize that I am part of a benevolent cycle, along with all trees and plants?

WE SHOULD NOTICE THAT WE ARE ALREADY SUPPORTED EVERY MOMENT. THERE IS THE EARTH BELOW OUR FEET AND THERE IS THE AIR, FILLING OUR LUNGS AND EMPTYING THEM. WE SHOULD BEGIN FROM THIS WHEN WE NEED SUPPORT.

NATALIE GOLDBERG

KNOW YOUR INTENTIONS

The Serenity Prayer was adopted into 12-step programs around the world in 1941: "God, grant me the serenity to accept the things I cannot change, the courage to change the things I can, and the wisdom to know the difference." It aims to deliver perspective when you experience fear in the face of what you cannot know or control.

The words of this prayer remind you that you can cultivate tranquility through surrender and rise to the challenging occasions of life through accessing courage. This kind of wisdom helps you face the many circumstances of not-knowing that you encounter every day.

When a wave of uncertainty arrives, greet it with graciousness and equanimity, knowing that courage and wisdom wait for you in the wings, available when you need them.

» What do I have the power to change now?

_____

_____

_____

_____

» What must I let be?

_____

_____

_____

_____

I GREETED UNCERTAINTY WITH CALMNESS TODAY.

★ ★ ★ ★ ★ ★

TREASURE YOUR BODY

When you revere life, you can better appreciate all that is extraordinary, functioning, and whole about your body. Celebrate what works, knowing it could always be otherwise. Staying mindful of the suffering of others can help you reframe your own. And what your body has endured may be the exact reframe that someone else needs to gain perspective. We are each other's teachers, keepers, healers. When you appreciate your own scars, you can respect the wounds of others. It has been wisely said: Be kind, for everyone you meet is fighting a hard battle.

Allow yourself to feel grateful for the countless aspects of your body that are working exquisitely in every moment.

» What parts of my body are working well right now?

_____

_____

_____

_____

_____

_____

_____

_____

_____

_____

TODAY I GRATEFULLY ACKNOWLEDGED SOME OF THE MANY
PRIVILEGES AND GIFTS OF MY BODY.

★ ★ ★ ★ ★ ★

IT'S WISE TO
ACCEPT THAT
HUMAN FAULTS
ARE INEVITABLE.
FACTOR THAT IN AND
KEEP GOING.

ALICE WALKER

What changes when I let go of expecting perfection?

FIND PLEASURE IN THE UNKNOWABLE

Without the existence of all that is mysterious, we would live only with what is known and knowable. Imagine how your life would shrink if everything unfolded exactly as you expected. How terribly one-dimensional it would be to construct and control everything. Instead, you have mystery to thank for the greatest joys and blessings in your life: its unexpected teachings, the lessons that choose you, the love from across the room, the new friends, the chance encounters with beauty and inspiration, the gift of another day.

Think of times when beauty, love, and joy have surprised you. Know that their shared home is uncertainty.

» Love surprised me when . . .

_____

_____

_____

_____

_____

_____

» Beauty surprised me when . . .

_____

_____

_____

_____

_____

_____

_____

» Joy surprised me when . . .

_____
_____
_____
_____
_____
_____
_____
_____
_____

» Inspiration surprised me when . . .

_____
_____
_____
_____
_____
_____
_____
_____
_____

» Relief surprised me when . . .

_____
_____
_____
_____
_____
_____
_____
_____

I WELCOMED SURPRISE TODAY.

★ ★ ★

★ ★ ★

★ ★ ★

★ ★ ★

A LIFE OF GRATITUDE ACCEPTS THE BAD WITH THE GOOD. GENUINE GRATITUDE IS NOT A ZERO-SUM GAME IN WHICH THANKFULNESS INCREASES THE MORE FORTUNATE YOU ARE AND DECREASES THE MORE ADVERSITY YOU EXPERIENCE.

DAN CLENDENIN

BE GRATEFUL EVEN WHEN NOT FEELING GREAT

When you're not feeling well, your absence of well-being can become your sole focus. You may be tempted to freely share your ills when people ask how you are doing. But constantly talking about what isn't working to the exclusion of those things that are working can reinforce a sense of being broken or alone.

When, instead, you acknowledge the full truth of how you are—holding wellness and illness, challenge and ease simultaneously—you send affirming messages to your body and mind. You also send a powerful message to the people around you, giving them permission to have and share the well-rounded truth of their own full experience.

When someone asks how you are doing, experiment with offering this response: "I am not feeling great, and I am still grateful." Or, "Not great, but grateful." Notice how this allows for more of everything to be true at once—you are not entirely one thing or another. Ask how the other person is feeling, too. Notice how your acknowledgment might impact their response.

» How do I feel when I speak more honestly about my true well-being?

_____

_____

_____

_____

_____

_____

_____

_____

_____

_____

APPRECIATE DIFFICULT EMOTIONS

If you look back on your life, you will see that there is no feeling you have not experienced in some form before. And survived. Or enjoyed. Mostly learned from if you have allowed yourself to take in its teachings. Each has made you who you are now. The surprises faced with courage, the pain met with tenderness, the challenges held with faith—they all make you more alive. It is often your most challenging emotional experiences that burnish you into brighter shining.

Remind yourself of tough situations and emotions that you did not expect but that made you who you are. Know that you will be able to look back on current struggles with appreciation for their teachings.

» What difficult emotions and situations have I learned from?

_____

_____

_____

_____

_____

_____

_____

_____

_____

_____

I APPRECIATED THE WISDOM OF DIFFICULT EMOTIONS.

★ ★ ★ ★ ★ ★

LIFE DOES NOT ACCOMMODATE YOU, IT SHATTERS YOU.... EVERY SEED DESTROYS ITS CONTAINER OR ELSE THERE WOULD BE NO FRUITION.

FLORIDA SCOTT-MAXWELL

SEE VARIETY AS A BLESSING

Your feelings serve you most when they are diversified, when your emotional landscape contains a range of terrains—all extraordinary. Variety is a blessing. The wider your capacities, the more resourceful you can be in all areas of your life. The more you can adapt and accommodate, the more resilient you are. The more emotions you can encounter and befriend, the more riches you have to bring to your life and the lives of others. Imagine how diminished you would be with only a single emotion through which to experience life.

Consider your emotions a privilege, each one able to bring richness to the landscape of your life when greeted with appreciation.

» I appreciate it when I feel joy because . . .

_____

_____

_____

_____

» I appreciate it when I feel sorrow because . . .

_____

_____

_____

_____

» I appreciate it when I feel fear because . . .

_____

_____

_____

_____

_____

» I appreciate it when I feel courage because . . .

_____

_____

_____

_____

_____

_____

_____

_____

» I appreciate it when I feel uplifted because . . .

_____

_____

_____

_____

_____

_____

_____

» I appreciate it when I feel sluggish because . . .

_____

_____

_____

_____

_____

_____

_____

_____

I BEFRIENDED MY EMOTIONS TODAY.

★ ★ ★

★ ★ ★

★ ★ ★

★ ★ ★

When I say to myself "My life is a gift," what feelings arise?

"I AM GIFT." ALL THAT I AM IS SOMETHING THAT'S GIVEN, AND GIVEN FREELY. BEING DOESN'T COST ANYTHING. THERE'S NO PRICE TAG, NO STRINGS ATTACHED.

THOMAS MERTON

WHEN PERFECTION EXISTS AS THE NATURE OF YOUR HEART, WHY DO YOU LOSE YOUR COMPOSURE BY DWELLING ON IMPERFECTIONS?

SRI RAMANA MAHARSHI

GIVE YOURSELF CREDIT

It is a radical act to acknowledge how whole and complete you are, especially within a culture bent on trying to convince you that you are not enough. It is a radical act of gratefulness to celebrate all that is abundant and extraordinary about you and your life. You can give yourself credit for resilience in the face of a life that is not always easy. You can affirm your courage and strength. You can delight in your idiosyncrasies that enrich the love that others feel toward you. And you can be grateful for the conditions that have allowed you to develop your extraordinary strengths.

» What are the ways that I am already enough?

I CELEBRATED MYSELF AS WHOLE AND COMPLETE,
JUST THE WAY THAT I AM.

TRUST IN LIFE

Look back to the times when you have placed your trust in life, when you have surrendered yourself to the flow of the river and let it carry you. It is very important that you build yourself a reliable index of memories of how life has made itself known to you as trustworthy, even if your mind quarrels with the concept. Your mind may gravitate to stockpiling memories of times when your fears were proven true or when life disappointed or hurt you, but the number of moments when life did not fail you far exceed those. Every time you follow your intuition, come through something difficult a little wiser, or let yourself be surprised by life's unfolding instead of controlling it, you give life a second chance. You have a 100 percent survival rate to date. This is all worthy reinforcement for putting your trust in life.

» I placed my trust in life when . . .

_____

_____

_____

_____

» I placed my trust in life when . . .

_____

_____

_____

_____

» I placed my trust in life when . . .

_____

_____

_____

» I placed my trust in life when . . .

_____

_____

_____

_____

_____

_____

_____

_____

_____

» I placed my trust in life when . . .

_____

_____

_____

_____

_____

_____

_____

_____

_____

» I placed my trust in life when . . .

_____

_____

_____

_____

_____

_____

_____

_____

I LET LIFE CARRY ME TODAY.

★ ★ ★

★ ★ ★

★ ★ ★

★ ★ ★

TURN ENVY AROUND

Envy is an important source of information about your longings, but it separates you from your contentment and can wreak havoc on your connections with others. Feeling inspired connects you with people whose lives embody what you desire. Whenever you experience a twinge of envy, turn it into inspiration. Practice noticing and saying to yourself, "I am so inspired by . . ." Become aware of how this shift impacts your sense of opportunity and possibility. As an added practice, tell a person who has helped you connect with one of your true longings how inspired you are by their example.

» I am so inspired by . . .

_____

_____

_____

» I am so inspired by . . .

_____

_____

_____

» I am so inspired by . . .

_____

_____

_____

» I am so inspired by . . .

_____

_____

_____

GIVING THANKS
CONSTANTLY AND IN
ALL CIRCUMSTANCES
LIBERATES US
FROM ENVY.

EDWARD HAYS

ACKNOWLEDGE EARTH'S GENEROSITY

The natural world is constantly providing you nourishment in both seen and unseen ways. There is such a glorious abundance surrounding you in every moment. No matter where you live, the Earth helps to keep you breathing. You can be inspired every time you open your heart and senses! You are provided food from the Earth's riches. Trees, plants, herbs, roots, water— all blessings. Even under threat, the Earth remains generous. Awakening to the extraordinary wonders and plenty of the natural world, you can be ever grateful.

When you are next enjoying a meal, reflect on the fact that all of the raw foods arose from the Earth. Think of how your nourishment is provided for. Say a blessing of thanksgiving.

» How has the natural world generously provided for me today?

_____

_____

_____

_____

_____

_____

_____

_____

_____

_____

_____

_____

EMBRACE THE INTANGIBLE

Everything you can touch is impermanent. Nothing you purchase will last. No matter how identified you are with the things you own, all objects are actually ephemeral and could be lost at any moment. Wake-up call experiences remind us of this, and you are lucky if you receive warnings and teachings as opposed to more significant losses. Fires, floods, storms, accidents—these are occasions when we are reminded of what really matters and endures.

Consider how you could look at all the stuff you own that would not survive a flood or fire, versus what will last beyond you.

» What matters most to me that cannot be "lost"?

_____

_____

_____

_____

_____

_____

_____

_____

_____

_____

_____

I TENDED TO THE GIFTS IN MY LIFE THAT MATTER MOST.

★ ★ ★ ★ ★ ★

SHIFT THE CONVERSATION TO SUFFICIENCY

When you find yourself in conversations that keep gravitating toward complaining or perseverating in unconstructive ways, try to make gentle shifts in the conversation. You can honor the human need for commiseration and compassion while also redirecting people toward noticing the resources we all have. The point of this practice is to change your language, not to change someone else's. Model what it can look like to be vulnerable and grateful at the same time. Challenge yourself to stop focusing on what might be lacking in your own life. Inspire others to notice the gifts in their lives by remarking on those you appreciate in yours. When you remind yourself of what you have going for you, you are better able to deal with what is not going your way.

» How could acknowledging more gratitude shift my conversations?

When there's a big disappointment, we don't know if that's the end of the story. It may just be the beginning of a great adventure.

PEMA CHÖDRÖN

RECOGNIZE THE GIFTS OF UNCERTAINTY

Spend a minute focusing on some of the things you know for sure. Tried-and-true formulas. Facts that hold up under scrutiny. You can search and confirm or disprove things as humans never have before in history. Technology offers you answers to longstanding questions in seconds. You can learn words in a new language with the help of your phone. How wonderful to have the privilege of certainty. And what a welcome, gracious privilege uncertainty can be, too.

Consider the places of uncertainty in your life as spacious pockets of respite from the work of knowing and having to know. Allow yourself to sink into the mysteries of life with appreciation.

» I know for sure that . . .

_____

_____

_____

» I appreciate the mystery of . . .

_____

_____

_____

» Accepting the unknown, I feel . . .

_____

_____

_____

TODAY I WAS GRATEFUL FOR THE MYSTERIES OF LIFE.

★ ★ ★ ★ ★ ★

BEHOLD YOURSELF AS A NEWBORN

One way to gain perspective is to look at yourself as if you were beholding a newborn; your essential nature is so much more available to you in infancy. Babies are reminders of the marvel of human life and also its fragility. To become and remain incarnate is nothing short of miraculous. If you can cherish yourself unconditionally the way you cherish a new life, you can know yourself anew. It can take your breath away to revel in your magnificence; yes, even in the midst of your messiness. If you allow yourself a larger field of appreciation, you will come to life more fully.

Let yourself be awestruck by the marvel of your existence. See yourself through eyes of wonder and through the warmth of your own embrace. Pick yourself up with love.

» When I consider the miracle of my existence, what feelings arise?

PART 3

AWAKEN POSSIBILITY

Possibility enlivens the moment at hand and animates your imagination and energy for what can be.

When opportunities knock, they rarely knock just once. They keep on arriving, and they all point us to possibility. Only when we are available to life can we hear and heed how we are called. Envisioning and investing in new possibilities is how transformation comes about. But how do we step into all the possibility that exists in a moment? We harness our big hearts and go forward with purposeful intention. We say "Yes!" to life.

CULTIVATE POSSIBILITY

Allow yourself to focus your attention on cultivating a sense of possibility. Notice what arises in you as you write or repeat the following prompts. Offer space for what wants to emerge, especially if a sense of hesitation comes up.

» My grateful heart moves me to . . .

_____

_____

_____

_____

_____

_____

_____

» Opportunity is beckoning me . . .

_____

_____

_____

_____

_____

_____

_____

_____

» Embracing my role in shaping what is possible . . .

_____

_____

_____

_____

_____

_____

_____

» Seeing life as a gift, I am moved to act on behalf of . . .

_____

_____

_____

_____

_____

_____

_____

» Emboldening my vision for the future, I . . .

_____

_____

_____

_____

_____

_____

_____

I CULTIVATED A SENSE OF POSSIBILITY TODAY.

★ ★ ★

★ ★ ★

★ ★ ★

★ ★ ★

GRATEFULIZE

Regularly letting people know that you notice them and they matter makes a huge difference—and this practice is highly contagious. It costs you nothing and has the potential to change everything. It is hard to get this one wrong if your grateful heart leads the way.

Make a list of people you tend to take for granted, or who have changed your life for the better and you never really let them know. Think of your many circles of connection—family, friends, colleagues, neighbors, acquaintances. Each day, choose at least one person to "gratefulize" in whatever way you are moved to do so—it could be through a note, an email, an e-card, a phone call, or a gesture of kindness in person. Make this a daily practice, and be as generous and specific with each person as you can be. Revel in the ripple effects.

DATE:_____ /_____ /_____

» Today, I will show _____ my gratitude by . . .

_____

_____

_____

DATE:_____ /_____ /_____

» Today, I will show _____ my gratitude by . . .

_____

_____

DATE:_____ /_____ /_____

» Today, I will show _____ my gratitude by . . .

_____

_____

Recipients of our APPRECIATION are APT TO express THEIR OWN GRATITUDE TO OTHERS, LENGTHENING THE UNENDING, GOLDEN CHAIN OF CONNECTIONS- IN-GOODNESS THAT STRETCHES ACROSS THE WORLD.

MARY FORD-GRABOWSKY

EXPERIMENT WITH THREE-WORD WONDERS

"I love you" is a potent gift if offered with sincerity. So are many other three-word phrases. Experiment with generating or deepening a conversation by using one of the three-word prompts below. For each prompt, write down the name of a person important to you and what you would say to them. Begin practicing with them, and witness what happens. Try these to offer the gifts of your humility and generosity to others.

» _____, I am grateful . . .

_____

_____

_____

» _____, I can see . . .

_____

_____

_____

» _____, I am wondering . . .

_____

_____

_____

» _____, help me understand . . .

_____

_____

_____

» _____, I am here . . .

_____

_____

_____

» _____, it makes sense . . .

_____

_____

_____

» _____, I can imagine . . .

_____

_____

_____

» _____, I am sorry . . .

_____

_____

_____

» _____, let's pause briefly . . .

_____

_____

_____

DO YOUR LITTLE BIT OF GOOD WHERE YOU ARE; IT'S THOSE LITTLE BITS OF GOOD PUT TOGETHER THAT OVERWHELM THE WORLD.

ARCHBISHOP DESMOND TUTU

When have I taken small steps with others in service of big changes?

LIVE FROM YOUR VALUES

What are your core values? Know what moves and motivates your actions so you can be guided by what matters most to you. Write down your guiding values or principles and keep them where you can be reminded of them throughout your day. When you act in alignment with these, you are standing for your deep convictions. When circumstances do not align with your convictions, the strength of your values will support you in knowing what to do.

How would you like these commitments to show up more powerfully as you think of yourself addressing the hurts around you and in the larger world? Lean into your values for guidance as you seek to live in greater alignment while having greater impact.

» What are my guiding values or principles?

1. _____

_____

_____

2. _____

_____

_____

3. _____

_____

_____

4. _____

_____

_____

5. _____

_____

» How can I live in greater alignment with my values?

_____

_____

_____

_____

_____

_____

_____

_____

_____

_____

_____

_____

_____

_____

_____

_____

_____

_____

I ACTED IN ALIGNMENT WITH MY CORE VALUES.

★ ★ ★ ★ ★

EMBODY YOUR COMMITMENT TO WELL-BEING

Many of us espouse strongly principled commitments to well-being and health. We say we care about and appreciate our physical selves. And yet what we say and where we actually put our time, attention, and energy may be very different. Be clear about what you value about your body, and then find ways to remember and act in alignment with these core beliefs. Living with appreciation and integrity enhances your perspective.

Clarify your values and principles regarding your body. Write them down. What guides you? Hold this guidance close whenever you tend your body.

» What do I value about my body? How can I act in alignment with these values?

_____

_____

_____

_____

_____

_____

_____

_____

_____

_____

_____

I TENDED MY BODY IN ALIGNMENT WITH MY VALUES.

★ ★ ★ ★ ★ ★

ENGAGE WITH YOUR VALUES

Find an organization doing work that advances your values. The focus could be on education, healthcare, civic engagement, social change, civil rights, environmental advocacy, or some other worthy cause. There are many ways to show your support—donating money and volunteering your time are only two. Consider bringing your creativity or outreach skills to the table. Attend events, write thank-you notes. Inquire as to what is needed, and then respond accordingly. These kinds of small daily investments multiply your efforts and effectiveness in helping to shape a thriving world.

» Where is my grateful support most needed right now?

» Who and what do I want to help thrive?

SERVE VULNERABILITY

Consider the ways your vulnerability could be a gift to others. Who needs to know that their vulnerability does not separate them from the rest of the world? Think of ways that you could share your vulnerability in support of an individual, group, or population in need. Tell your story. Offer yourself in service. Make a commitment to show up in places where the truth of vulnerability is a shared norm—for people struggling with addictions, mental health issues, poverty, illness, or human tenderness.

» What aspects of myself am I most at ease sharing with the world?

_____

_____

_____

» What aspects of myself have I made less welcome?

_____

_____

_____

_____

» How and where can I show up with my vulnerability as a gift to others?

_____

_____

_____

_____

I SHARED MY VULNERABILITY WITH OTHERS.

★ ★ ★ ★ ★

WHEN I DARE TO BE
POWERFUL,
TO USE MY
STRENGTH
IN THE SERVICE OF MY
VISION, THEN IT
BECOMES LESS AND
LESS IMPORTANT
WHETHER I AM AFRAID.

AUDRE LORDE

GIVE YOURSELF GRATEFULLY

When you relate to yourself generously, there is far more of yourself to offer; the time and energy you previously spent in various forms of mistrust and mistreatment of yourself can now be used to help others. Choose one way you can be of service this week, and do it fully and gratefully, feeling blessed by the opportunity to give. Listen to your need for self-care, and trust that you will offer it to yourself as needed. Watch how much further you can extend yourself and how much more you can give when self-trust and great fullness of heart guide you.

DATE:_____ /_____ /_____

» This week, I will be of service fully and gratefully . . .

_____

_____

_____

DATE:_____ /_____ /_____

» This week, I will be of service fully and gratefully . . .

_____

_____

_____

DATE:_____ /_____ /_____

» This week, I will be of service fully and gratefully . . .

_____

_____

_____

DATE:_____ /_____ /_____

» This week, I will be of service fully
   and gratefully . . .

_____

_____

_____

_____

_____

_____

_____

DATE:_____ /_____ /_____

» This week, I will be of service fully
   and gratefully . . .

_____

_____

_____

_____

_____

_____

_____

DATE:_____ /_____ /_____

» This week, I will be of service fully
   and gratefully . . .

_____

_____

_____

_____

_____

_____

_____

**I SERVED MYSELF AS I
SERVED OTHERS.**

★ ★ ★

★ ★ ★

★ ★ ★

★ ★ ★

EVEN IF YOU HAVE A LOT OF WORK TO DO, IF YOU THINK OF IT AS WONDERFUL, AND IF YOU FEEL IT AS WONDERFUL, IT WILL TRANSFORM INTO THE ENERGY OF JOY AND FIRE INSTEAD OF BECOMING A BURDEN.

TULKU THONDUP RINPOCHE

�֎

If I think of my work today as wonderful, what energizes me?

DATE:_____ /_____ /_____

_____

_____

_____

_____

_____

If I think of my work today as wonderful, what energizes me?

DATE:_____ /_____ /_____

_____

_____

_____

_____

_____

If I think of my work today as wonderful, what energizes me?

DATE:_____ /_____ /_____

_____

_____

_____

_____

_____

VALUE THE EARTH

Most of us have daily behaviors that express our values about the environment. You might recycle cans and bottles, bring reusable bags to the grocery store, or use biodegradable products. Maybe you belong to a food co-op or buy from your local farmers' market. Additionally, it is important to consider what else you might need to do to be in alignment with your values. What truly matters to you? How do you offer your attention and appreciation to what matters most?

Know that every little thing you do and choice you make can take you into or out of alignment with your value of the Earth's well-being. Commit to doing a little more to better love what you value, and value what you love.

DATE:_____ / _____ / _____

» Because I value the Earth's well-being, today I will . . .

_____

_____

DATE:_____ / _____ / _____

» Because I value the Earth's well-being, today I will . . .

_____

_____

DATE:_____ / _____ / _____

» Because I value the Earth's well-being, today I will . . .

_____

_____

I MADE A POINT TO RECYCLE.

★ ★ ★ ★ ★

I WALKED, BIKED, OR TOOK PUBLIC TRANSPORTATION WHEN I COULD.

★ ★ ★ ★ ★

I BROUGHT A REUSABLE SHOPPING BAG TO THE STORE.

★ ★ ★ ★ ★

I TOOK A SHORTER SHOWER.

★ ★ ★ ★ ★

I UNPLUGGED ALL OF MY DEVICES WHEN I WAS DONE USING THEM.

★ ★ ★ ★ ★

GO TO A SPECIAL SPACE

Imagine yourself somewhere that awakens your sense of communion with the glories of our Earth. What spot on our planet gives rise to a feeling of peace and well-being for you? Give this place a name. What do you most appreciate about this place? What do you notice when you are there? Look up. Look down. Describe both the distant landscape and the details you see if you look closely. What is your felt sense of this place? What feelings arise when you imagine being here?

When you have a strong sense of a place you would call "home," think about the kinds of things that threaten this spot. What kinds of forces is this place susceptible to? Are there things that imperil the sustainability of this place? When you imagine the sacred places you are grateful for, as well as their vulnerability, what do you feel inspired to do to protect them? Think of some small acts to protect the world you cherish. Now think of how you could go and act on them.

» How can I protect the places I most appreciate?

The more that we deeply appreciate, care for, and feel inextricably tied to the places, things, and people of this world, the more we are likely to TAKE A STAND on behalf of WHAT WE VALUE.

KRISTI NELSON

BE A CITIZEN RATHER THAN A CONSUMER

Living with gratefulness, you can commit to living in ways that leave a lighter footprint, consume fewer nonrenewable resources, allocate money in alignment with your values, and unleash generosity. When you act merely as a consumer, you stop behaving like a citizen who can have an impact with your time, choices, and resources. When you live by your principles and tend what you value, a sense of felt sufficiency frees you up to consider the needs of others and to participate in shaping the world in which you live.

Consider how you could more deeply align your lifestyle choices with your core values and have a greater experience of sufficiency.

DATE: _____ / _____ / _____

» How can I shape the world with values-aligned choices today?

_____

_____

_____

_____

DATE: _____ / _____ / _____

» How can I shape the world with values-aligned choices today?

_____

_____

_____

_____

I MADE A POSITIVE IMPACT WITH MY TIME, CHOICES, OR
RESOURCES TODAY.

★ ★ ★ ★ ★

BE PART OF SOMETHING LARGER

Believing that we each have the capacity for impact, thoughtful, committed citizens have long made it their business to change the world for the better. Surprising acts have changed the course of history: the stand-offs in Tiananmen Square, the opposition to apartheid in South Africa, the pipeline protests at Standing Rock, the nonviolent resistance of the American civil rights movement. The collective includes each of us.

Consider yourself one among many thoughtful, committed citizens, who—in small ways, over time—have shifted the dial. Surprise yourself with your vision and courage.

» How can I act in service of a movement for change I wish to see in the world?

DRAW ON A WELLSPRING OF LOVE

Sit quietly and connect with love and the fullness of your heart. Visualize this wellspring as an inexhaustible source inside you. Just as you would heed love to direct you to tend the hurts of a child, you can heed love to direct you to tend needs on a larger scale. Let yourself know that the more love that pours out of your heart, the more your heart will fill up with love.

» How is love moving me to tend the hurts in the world?

I LET LOVE GUIDE ME TODAY.

» How is my grateful heart filling me up?

_____

_____

_____

_____

_____

_____

_____

_____

» What opportunities invite me to offer love?

_____

_____

_____

_____

_____

_____

_____

_____

_____

THAT'S WHAT I CONSIDER TRUE GENEROSITY: YOU GIVE YOUR ALL, AND YET YOU ALWAYS FEEL AS IF IT COSTS YOU NOTHING.

SIMONE DE BEAUVOIR

How can I give my "all" today?

DATE:_____ /_____ /_____

_____
_____
_____
_____
_____

How can I give my "all" today?

DATE:_____ /_____ /_____

_____
_____
_____
_____
_____

How can I give my "all" today?

DATE:_____ /_____ /_____

_____
_____
_____
_____
_____

USE YOUR BLESSINGS

It is only when you claim the blessings you have that you can make use of them to have an impact—not from a place of guilt but from appreciative responsibility. Your ordinary is truly someone else's extraordinary. If you have money (even a little) and you are thankful, you can put it to use and share it. If you have a body that works, you can count yourself fortunate, help get things done, help others, and offer care. If you have education, strengths, or skills, they are gifts longing to be uplifted and of use.

Think about how resources that are sufficient in your life could be of use to the larger world. Only when you recognize and fully acknowledge your plenty can you make a difference with what you have.

DATE:_____ /_____ /_____

» If I felt that I truly had and were enough, what would I offer freely today?

_____

_____

_____

_____

_____

DATE:_____ /_____ /_____

» If I felt that I truly had and were enough, what would I share freely today?

_____

_____

_____

_____

_____

Gratitude is LIBERATING. IT IS SUBVERSIVE. IT HELPS US REALIZE THAT WE ARE SUFFICIENT, AND THAT REALIZATION FREES US.

JOANNA MACY

TAKE A STAND FOR WHAT MATTERS

Times of upheaval call on us to know what we stand for and compel us to act with courage on behalf of those values. When your core values are in discord with what you see around you, it is vital to deepen your commitment to your principles, to make sure that they are explicit and unequivocal in your heart, articulated in your life, and expressed with clarity when called for. Knowing what you stand for helps you to know very clearly what you will not stand for, and vice versa. Tending to the principles you appreciate most is empowering and enlightening.

Live like a tuning fork, able to sense whether what is happening around you is in or out of harmony with what you value. Take a stand when your core principles are compromised.

» What are five of my core principles?

1. _____

_____

2. _____

_____

3. _____

_____

4. _____

_____

5. _____

_____

» What is compromising those principles?

_____

_____

_____

_____

_____

_____

» How might I take a stand?

_____

_____

_____

_____

_____

_____

_____

_____

I TOOK A STAND FOR WHAT MATTERS.

★ ★ ★ ★ ★ ★

NOTICE THE REVERBERATIONS OF LEGACY

If legacy is the culmination of our choices, everyone who has ever lived has left a legacy of some kind. People such as Anne Frank leave a legacy with significant reverberations even though they lived only a short time. It does not take a long life to leave a substantive legacy, but it takes intention. We could also say that many of the people who left legacies that have impacted us and the world the most are those who were able to find ways to be grateful for the gifts and opportunities available to them, taking a stand for what mattered most to them, even in the most trying or short-lived circumstances.

Think of some of the people whose legacies have inspired you the most and consider their common characteristics. Become more aware of the inspiration available to you.

» What are some common characteristics of the people whose legacies have inspired me? How might I act on this inspiration?

MAKE VISIBLE WHAT, WITHOUT YOU, MIGHT PERHAPS NEVER HAVE BEEN SEEN.

ROBERT BRESSON

Be the most ethical, the most responsible, the most authentic you can be with every breath you take, because you are cutting a path into tomorrow that others will follow.

KEN WILBER

SHAPE YOUR LEGACY

Your legacy is made from the choices you make, and at their best they will reflect your deep beliefs and core values. When you live gratefully, you are continually oriented and reoriented toward ways of being that fortify the heart: generosity, compassion, reverence, respect, humility, joy, and more. These are the kinds of words you will want etched on your tombstone and in the hearts of those who will remember you after you have gone.

Imagine yourself remembered for the qualities that you hold most dear, and make choices today that will help you to be who you want to be memorialized for being.

» What qualities do I want to be remembered for?

_____

_____

_____

_____

_____

» What choices can I make today to help shape the legacy I want to leave?

_____

_____

_____

_____

_____

TODAY I MADE A CHOICE THAT WILL HELP SHAPE THE LEGACY
I WANT TO LEAVE.

★ ★ ★ ★ ★ ★

GIVE THE ULTIMATE LEGACY OF LOVE

Joyful memory is the terrain of joyful legacy. It is what will sustain you in profound ways as you make meaning of your life in your final years, and it will sustain your loved ones once you are gone. There is no legacy greater than love. And there is also no opportunity to bring forth greater pleasure than how you show your love. No matter what, the love and care you leave in the hearts of others will be what you are remembered for. Love has staying power. Love is transformative. Your love for life will be the indelible signature you leave behind, and with it will be all of the hearts you have signed with your affection.

Consider where the threads of joyful connection are strong in your life, and where they could be strengthened. Let cultivating love today be your grateful living legacy.

DATE:_____ /_____ /_____

» Today, to cultivate love, I will . . .

_____

_____

_____

_____

DATE:_____ /_____ /_____

» Today, to cultivate love, I will . . .

_____

_____

_____

_____

DATE:_____ /_____ /_____

» Today, to cultivate love, I will . . .

_____

_____

_____

_____

DATE:_____ /_____ /_____

» Today, to cultivate love, I will . . .

_____

_____

_____

_____

DATE:_____ /_____ /_____

» Today, to cultivate love, I will . . .

_____

_____

_____

_____

TODAY, I STRENGTHENED A THREAD OF JOYFUL CONNECTION.

★ ★ ★ ★ ★ ★

STICKERS AND POP-OUT TOOLS
FOR EXPANDING YOUR PRACTICE

In the following pages, you will find fun stickers and pop-outs to help boost your daily gratitude practice. Use them to remind yourself and others that life is worthy of cherishing and celebrating. Bring them into your day in creative ways:

- **Use the star stickers** to fill in the star prompts in the previous pages. Each time you do what is written, give yourself a star!

- **Post the affirmation stickers** on your mirror, computer, or fridge or in your car or anywhere you will see them regularly.

- **Use the bookmarks** to keep your place in this workbook, or use them in another book as a gentle reminder to focus on gratitude.

- **Send the postcards** to friends to boost their spirits, or make a greeting card from them.

- **Let one of the mini quote cards** guide your meditation practice for a period of time.

- **Use any of the quotes** as prompts for a morning writing practice, journaling, a poem, or a story.

- **Let a quote** inspire you to take a photograph or be creative in order to capture its essence.

- **Put the conversation starters** in a bowl or basket where you can choose one to focus on each day.

- **Use one conversation starter** each day to catalyze a conversation at mealtime.

HOW WONDERFUL IT IS THAT NOBODY NEED WAIT A SINGLE MOMENT BEFORE STARTING TO IMPROVE THE WORLD.

ANNE FRANK

TO BE ASTONISHED IS ONE OF THE SUREST WAYS OF NOT GROWING OLD TOO QUICKLY.

SIDONIE-GABRIELLE COLETTE

THERE IS NO GREATER MISTAKE THAN TO TRY TO LEAP AN ABYSS IN TWO JUMPS.

DAVID LLOYD GEORGE

WHEREVER YOU ARE IS THE ENTRY POINT

KABIR

WALLS TURNED SIDEWAYS ARE BRIDGES.

ANGELA DAVIS

MAY YOU LIVE ALL THE DAYS OF YOUR LIFE.

JONATHAN SWIFT

LET ME FALL IF I MUST. THE ONE I WILL BECOME WILL CATCH ME.

BAAL SHEM TOV

STICKS IN A BUNDLE CANNOT BE BROKEN.

EAST AFRICAN PROVERB

HOW YOU DO **ANYTHING** IS HOW YOU DO **EVERY-THING.**

CHERI HUBER

HAPPINESS IS NOT A MATTER OF INTENSITY BUT OF **BALANCE** AND ORDER AND RHYTHM AND HARMONY.

THOMAS MERTON

ATTENTION IS THE **DOORWAY** TO GRATITUDE, THE DOORWAY TO WONDER, THE DOORWAY TO RECIPROCITY.

ROBIN WALL KIMMERER

HOW WE SPEND OUR **DAYS** IS, OF COURSE, HOW WE SPEND OUR **LIVES.**

ANNIE DILLARD

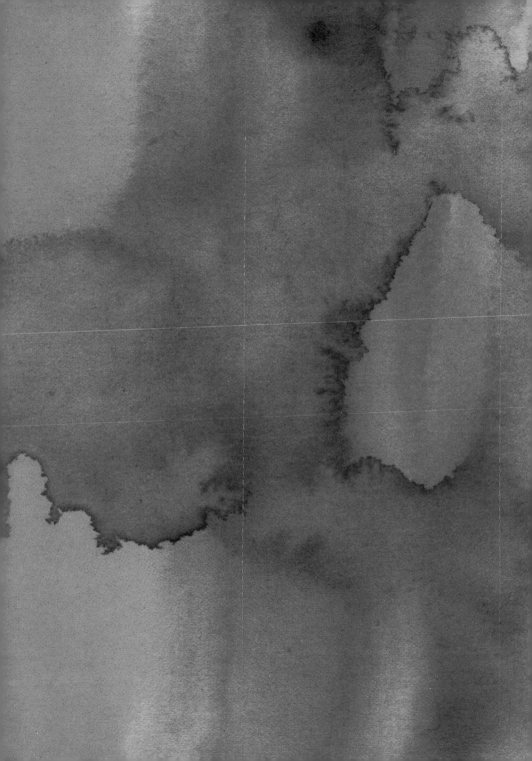

THE THINGS THAT FRIGHTEN US JUST WANT TO BE HELD.

MARK NEPO

THE UNIVERSE IS FULL OF MAGICAL THINGS PATIENTLY WAITING FOR OUR WITS TO GROW SHARPER.

EDEN PHILLPOTTS

SHOULD YOU SHIELD THE CANYONS FROM THE WINDSTORMS YOU WOULD NEVER SEE THE TRUE BEAUTY OF THEIR CARVINGS.

ELISABETH KÜBLER-ROSS

PEACE, LIKE MOST BEAUTIFUL THINGS, BEGINS SMALL.

SHANE CLAIBORNE,
JONATHAN WILSON-HARTGROVE
& ENUMA OKORO

WAKE AT DAWN WITH A WINGED HEART AND GIVE THANKS FOR ANOTHER DAY OF LOVING.

KAHLIL GIBRAN

THOSE WHO ARE AWAKE LIVE IN A CONSTANT STATE OF AMAZEMENT.

JACK KORNFIELD

THE WILLINGNESS TO CONSIDER POSSIBILITY REQUIRES A TOLERANCE OF UN-CERTAIN-TY.

RACHEL NAOMI REMEN

GIVE THANKS FOR UNKNOWN BLESSINGS ALREADY ON THEIR WAY.

NATIVE AMERICAN PROVERB

WHEREVER YOU GO, GO WITH **ALL YOUR HEART.**

CONFUCIUS

ASK TO KNOW WHAT YOU ARE BORN TO DO. FOLLOW THE **COMPASS** OF **JOY.**

BARBARA MARX HUBBARD

FOR ME, LOSING... ISN'T FAILURE, IT'S RESEARCH.

BILLIE JEAN KING

GRACe IS THE ABILITY TO **ReDEFINE** THE **BOUNDARIES** OF **POSSIBILITY.**

MANNING MARABLE

THE STORE WAS CLOSED SO I WENT HOME AND *hugged* WHAT I OWN.

BROOKS PALMER

IT'S THAT KNIFE-EDGE OF UNCERTAINTY WHERE WE COME ALIVE TO OUR TRUEST POWER.

JOANNA MACY

THIS IS TRUE HUMILITY: NOT THINKING LESS OF OURSELVES BUT THINKING OF OURSELVES LESS.

RICK WARREN

OPPORTUNITIES, MANY TIMES, ARE SO SMALL THAT WE GLIMPSE THEM NOT AND YET THEY ARE OFTEN THE SEEDS OF GREAT ENTERPRISES.

OG MANDINO

What are some obligations or responsibilities in your life you would like to appreciate more?

What do you have enough of?

What do you have more than enough of that you might share?

What helps you expand your perspective?

How does acknowledging your privileges and plenty make you feel more grateful?

How does opening to pleasure open you to greater appreciation?

What are some qualities in yourself you have judged that you could instead appreciate as lovable?

What are a few things you have had to lose or let go of in order to gain what you now treasure?

How have your losses made you appreciate what you have?

In what ways has growing older helped you to take less for granted?

When have you experienced kindness and thoughtfulness while navigating loss?

How can you liberate yourself from dwelling on imperfections?

What changes when you count your blessings?

How could you turn a source of envy into a source of inspiration?

In what ways could greater fullness of heart help you navigate your life as it is?

What opportunity is beckoning for your attention?

What do you have that is longing to be more appreciated?

Where does your loving heart want to overflow—and in service of what?

How does living in alignment with your values remind you to be grateful?

What helps you cultivate a sense of possibility in your life?

What helps you say "Yes!" to possibility?

How could you offer a fearful person support from a place of compassion and courage?

How might appreciating your own body increase your empathy and compassion for the struggles of others?

What emotions move you toward action?

If you were to treat yourself exactly as you long to, what might change?

Who in your life reminds you of the true gifts and opportunities of relationship?

What are some things you might say to offer appreciation to those whose relationships you value?

What are some habits, patterns, or beliefs that steal your capacity to be fully present in your relationships?

What commitments can you make to increase your availability to those you love?

Understanding inquiry as a form of generosity, what are some questions that help others know you are truly interested?

How do you embody humility in your relationships?

How might you be more generous with what you have?

How can you stretch yourself with more generosity toward people you have been anxious about connecting with?

How does grief open you to feel more connected to others?

What could you do to make grief a less isolating experience?

What are some ways that you currently demonstrate and share your love for our planet?

What more could you do to show grateful care for the Earth?

How can you let love guide you today to make a difference in your world?

How could you make it an art to approach everything you see and do from your heart?

When you feel grateful for someone or something, what kinds of actions does this inspire?

How could living and acting from gratitude make a healing difference in your community?

How are your actions likely to be different when they come from gratitude, rather than guilt or obligation?

How does it feel to act from a place of contentment?

How does the notion of legacy move or motivate you?

What changes when you remember that you are living your legacy now?

What can you do today to nurture one new possibility for the life and legacy you are living?

What could you do to nurture one new possibility for life after you are no longer here—your future legacy?

What does it mean to you to cultivate greater aliveness?

What are some of the ways you can prioritize and nurture what enlivens you?

When you are facing something uncertain in life, what words or actions help you stay present and persevere?

When you slow down, settle into stillness, and regard your body as your one true home, what sensations and feelings arise?

What aspect of your body are you aware of feeling most grateful for in this moment?

What about your body makes you feel a sense of awe?

What parts of your body want to be held with empathy?

What is an emotion you experience often and welcome with open arms?

What are some ways you could invite yourself to be more curious and compassionate when your emotions are challenging?

When you accept something—even if it does not feel easy or acceptable—how does this help you better learn from it?

What are things you can count on to bring you true contentment?

How can you invite greater trust into your life?

What does it mean to you to live wholeheartedly?